Tales of the Weddinglike Thing

In Which the Large Main Bride and the Small Auxiliary Backup Bride Survive Their Own Wedding

Jessica Weissman

December 2014

Street to Street
Epic Publications

Tales of the Weddinglike Thing: In Which the Large Main Bride and the Small Auxiliary Backup Bride Survive Their Own Wedding is published by Street to Street Epic Publications, Washington, DC, under the direction of Dr. Carolivia Herron.

Text copyright © 2014 by Jessica Weissman
Cover designed by Carolivia Herron

All rights reserved under International and Pan-American Copyright Conventions.
Published in the United States by Street to Street Epic Publications, Washington, DC.

www.carolivia.com
StreetToStreet.org
www.EpicCenterStories.org

Library of Congress Cataloging-in-Publication Data
Weissman, Jessica
Tales of the Weddinglike Thing: In Which the Large Main Bride and the Small Auxiliary Backup Bride Survive Their Own Wedding

Summary: In 1997 there was no legal same-sex marriage, and thus no weddings for two women. Louise and Jessica decide to call their commitment ceremony the Weddinglike Thing, or WLT. Laugh with them them as they prepare for the WLT with assistance from family and friends, including their deceased mothers who help them find the right shoes and a good deal on wine from beyond the grave.

Paper ISBN: 978-1-938609-27-5
Ebook ISBN: 978-1-938609-28-2

Dedicated to

Maud Hart Lovelace

and her devoted readers

Author's Note: This is a memoir, as true and accurate as I can make it, told for humorous effect. But I am looking through my own eyes, from my own point of view. Others may remember things differently, or with different emphasis.

Contents

THE BEGINNING   6

JUNE 4, 1996   8

WLT PREPARATIONS   9

JANUARY 29, 1997	9
FEBRUARY 3, 1997	10
FEBRUARY 11, 1997	10
MARCH 3, 1997	12
MARCH 5, 1997	13
MARCH 8, 1997	14
MARCH 19, 1997	15
MARCH 22, 1997	15
MARCH 23, 1987	15
MARCH 24, 1997	16
MARCH 26, 1997	18

MORE WLT PROGRESS   19

APRIL 1, 1997	19
APRIL 3, 1997	20
APRIL 7, 1997	20
APRIL 14, 1997	21
APRIL 20, 1997	22
APRIL 28, 1997	23

WLT PROGRESS   24

MAY 1, 1997	25
MAY 5, 1997	26
MAY 7, 1997	26
MAY 10, 1997	27

MAY 12, 1997	28
MAY 13, 1997	30
MAY 14, 1997	30
MAY 15, 1997	32
MAY 16, 1997	33
MAY 18, 1997	34

THE WLT ITSELF 38

MAY 18, 1997	38
MAY 26, 1997	40

POSTLUDE 44

JUNE 1, 1997	44
JUNE 7, 1997	44
JULY 4, 1997	46
JULY 14, 1997	49
JULY 31, 1997	50
AUGUST 15, 1997	50

ACKNOWLEDGEMENTS 52

ABOUT THE AUTHOR 53

Tales of the Weddinglike Thing

The Beginning

This is the story of how Louise and I survived our commitment ceremony, told in real time as it happened in the form of postings to an email listserv dedicated to fans of Maud Hart Lovelace's Betsy-Tacy books. Maud-L was, and still is, a tightly-knit group of articulate and interesting women who discussed this compelling series of books that takes its heroines from when they meet at age 5 until the last of the group marries. There are a few references that make more sense if you know the books. If you're confused by any of them, I heartily recommend that you find and read these beautifully written books set at the turn of the 20th century.

I met Louise in April 1996, after a series of misadventures in life and in love. An extended trip with a friend to India, Italy, England and Portugal ended in dual disasters in 1995: the friend and I no longer spoke and my girlfriend, who had a disease that made her connective tissue weak, died of a burst aorta.

At the suggestion of my bereavement group, I looked in the Washington Blade for a personal ad to answer. This was intended as a distraction, not as the start of a serious hunt for a partner. But it would get me out of the house for something other than work and cultural events.

The ad that caught my eye was distinctively straightforward and unapologetic. Either it was written by the woman's friends, or she was totally obnoxious. Or both. Here is how it read:

Skinny white woman with an attitude in search of a full-figured woman with a library and a sense of humor. Must be willing to be interviewed by a committee of my closest friends.

I draw a veil over the courtship and its slow rise. Neither of us intended anything more than being casual company to the other. How that changed and how we realized that we wanted to have some kind of public commitment is of much more interest to us than it could possibly be to anybody else.

Jessica Weissman

At some point we began referring to ourselves as the Large Main Bride and the Small Auxiliary Backup Bride.

So the story picks up here, with the planning of the Weddinglike Thing, or WLT. But first, here is how my Betsy-Tacy friends learned about the upcoming event. I was responding to someone wailing about the creative last name her cousin acquired.

Tales of the Weddinglike Thing

June 4, 1996

Katie, no need to feel sorry because your gay cousin is stuck with that last name you describe as horrible. I noticed you didn't tell us what it was so we could groan with you.

Anyway, plenty of lesbians change their birth names, often in ways that make me cringe but make them happy (lots of mystical last names like Mountainwater or Rainbow or StrongWomyn). And if she becomes partnered she and her partner may contemplate combining their names or taking a new one to confirm their entry into that state. I know the last because, much to my astonishment and abounding joy, at the age of 44, I am entering into precisely that contemplation with Louise. Unfortunately we can't think of anything to do with Kelley and Weissman that doesn't sound like a vaudeville act.

Suggestions are welcome.

Jessica Weissman

WLT Preparations

January 29, 1997

We have a celebrant, a good friend of mine who has done plenty of liturgies and who knows us. She isn't Jewish but is married to one, and is sufficiently conversant with traditional Jewish practice to help us blend that with what's possible for a WLT. Louise wants to have a ketubah, but hasn't quite grasped that it should be in Hebrew (or Aramaic, actually). So we may devise something similar that can be in English and framed and all that.

We are going out with the friend who will make the dresses today to see possibilities, too. She used to work at the Neiman Marcus down the street from my office, and thus can get us into the relevant parts of the store without annoying the sales force because we won't buy anything. I have to remember to dress presentably today.

So, invitations are next. Yikes! And registering at Crate and Barrel and other places that take nontraditional registrations. Of course I already have all the housewares I want and like, and that reflect my taste perfectly. Now I get to share with someone else with independent taste about all this. We got through selecting a stainless flatware pattern, but thats only because I don't care much about stainless flatware and will continue to use my battered antique plate. When it comes to dishes, who knows what will ensue. I'm told by experienced predecessors that no matter how reasonable we mean to be, there'll be something we end up projecting all other disagreements on. Good thing we don't have much in the way to disagreement to project (or at least so I think now).

And I'm digging my feet in about no Pachelbel Canon or Adagio for Strings.

Tales of the Weddinglike Thing
February 3, 1997

Well, ladies, I have cravenly given in completely on the matter of shoes for the WLT. Louise is now officially allowed to pick out anything that comes in wide and has less than two inch heels. We may end up with dye-to-match shoes that have additional handmade decorations. We may end up with something as yet unimagined on this planet. But I have agreed beforehand, a priori and without let or hindrance to wear them, no matter what.

In return I have gotten my way on not having a live band for the dancing portion of the afternoon. String quartet before and during the transition period, nothing much for a while, then a reliable disk jockey playing real rock (IE what I liked when I was in high school) for a while. Also no dorky floral centerpieces, esp. since we won't have assigned seats for people to occupy with their buffet food (high-style finger food is the plan). There will be two identical buffet tables, so that one picky or slow person can't hold up everybody. We'll also let people form two lines at each table, one on each side.

Invitations go out in ten days. You're all invited. Anybody who thinks she is likely to come, please send me your address and I'll send you a real paper invitation. May 18th, 2pm, in a large backyard in Fairfax, VA.

February 11, 1997
AMAZING FACT FOR TODAY

My apartment sold after 3 days on the market! After spending a frantic two weeks tiling and painting and moving things around and putting half my books and all my pictures in boxes in the basement and cleaning like a maniac and even, at the last minute, going to the hardware store to get a new toilet roller because a presumably resentful cat had knocked the previous one irretrievably under the sofa, we had an open house on Saturday and got two offers on Sunday night.

The open house fell during DC's first significant snow, which probably helped since it turned the view out my back windows into a glorious wonderland of snow on houses and trees. The best part, among many best parts, is that we got it sold before we had to move the file cabinet out of the bedroom into the basement. This would have been a huge burden, and we were putting it off until after the open house.

This despite the fact that the toad-head downstairs had an open house on the same day and kept trying to get people NOT to go upstairs to see mine as well. He is doing For Sale By Owner, because he thinks that the only reason realtors couldn't sell his apartment in six months is that they don't know their own business. Clearly he knows better, at least in his own mind.

Anyway, enough about Jeremiah.

Several spiffy and affordable new listings have come on the market and we will go out and look on Saturday, and probably make a decision the week after. So I should be out of the place I have lived in for twelve years and in a new home by April 15th or so. Kind of hard, since this apartment is my first true adult home (yes, I moved here in my early 30s and don't mean to discount my years in Delaware entirely, but take my word for it).

Now to choose among:

- the perfect tiny house with the kitchen with the bay window in it that has, alas, only one bathroom and no basement
- the large adorable Tudor that's not near enough to Metro (although the bus is one block away
- the Dutch Colonial in the historic area of Takoma Park that is lovely but overpriced
- the underimproved row house that's three blocks from my office but is priced at the top of our range
- the house down the street from some friends that has a kitchen in need of improvement but is priced low enough that we could just redo the kitchen
- the large elegant apartment two blocks from my current one with the view of the stone-walled azalea garden

Tales of the Weddinglike Thing

>   and no dumb old maintenance work ever, but doesn't allow cats
> - the schizophrenic house that is Tudor traditional downstairs and has a totally redone modern upstairs with a Southwestern theme and a one-person Jacuzzi in the bathtub
> - or....or....or....some other one we see tomorrow or next week

March 3, 1997

I went with my friend the seamstress to the Mecca of All Serious Sewing in the DC Area, a temple known as G Street Fabrics. This place is absolutely overwhelming, with 3 floors of fabric, 87 kinds of fancy lace, 82 shades of linen, and many many other esoteric fabric-related things, some of which I didn't even recognize.

After I recovered from my Past Life Regression into 8th grade sewing class, we did some serious looking, and found two shades of gorgeous jewel tone Thai silk (purple and a kind of blue), plus some amazing purple and gold lace to be used for a little wedge in the front of the bodices. Purple and gold lace SOUNDS hideous, but is actually lovely in small amounts and the proper application. I was cheered to discover that there actually IS something called Chantilly Lace. The Big Bopper knew whereof he spoke, or sang.

So, we are going to wear tailored silk jackets with lace vest-bodice things showing, and ripply skirts. This is all subject to Louise's approval, but I suspect we have it. The jackets will be wearable later on for other things. The bodice/vest things will be suitable for no other application. The skirts may or may not be re-wearable. If not, we'll get some matching pants made by the same seamstress friend.

If anybody wants me to, I can get the technically correct terms for all these things from the seamstress friend.

WHEW!

Jessica Weissman

March 5, 1997

Things are happening fast and furious. Our Miss Mix and I went back to the fabric store, picked out some fabulous lace together (deep purple with some sequins, far less tacky than it sounds and boy howdy will it catch the light). The fabric lady played right along with us, and as she was cutting the lace, whispered "this is for your wedding, no? I cut HERE then" and slid the scissors an inch or two further along. So we'll have some to glue to the shoes if that's what we want. Probably the first lace-encrusted Birkenstocks in the world.

We also got several zillion yards of truly frou-frou chiffon, but I balked at braving the Counter of the Button Ladies to select buttons. All the buttons look alike to me anyway, and I refuse to be taken in and have to choose among them. I don't care unless I can have 3-D Glitter Flintstones Buttons. Which don't seem to exist.

We ran out of time to select the fusible interfacing (which sounds to me like something I can use in my current Visual Basic program, but I'm assured it is not). We're not even talking linings yet.

Having survived the fabric mecca and the subsequent cheesecake at the cafe located strategically next to the fabric place, we called tent renters. Two or three will bid for our business.

On Saturday morning we are talking with the friend who will organize the food. We each made up lists of our desires for high-style finger food, and when you removed the unKosher items from Louise's, they mainly agree. And it looks like I will get my dream idea of two identical buffet tables, to cut down on pointless waiting.

This all may yet come off well. I have to get measured on Saturday afternoon, which will probably recall my stint as an experimental body. We had created a computer-based training lesson on how to measure for tailoring, which some of the home economics majors apparently didn't already know. To test the achievement of traditionally trained students versus the ones who had taken our on-line course, the professor ran a controlled experiment with students measuring real bodies, including mine. The best part was that they insisted on having refreshments, with cold cuts individually rolled on the tray. Unfortunately there's no way to include "Test Body" on ones professional resume without inducing unpleasant inquiries.

March 8, 1997

We finally have all components of the outfits bought, except for the buttons. I had NO idea how many different types of shoulder pads and interfacing our wonderful world embraces, nor did I know how long a dedicated dress designer can spend selecting among what seem to me to be several identical vest patterns. Once again I snapped after 45 minutes in the fabric mecca, so we just bought one each of the several exquisite buttons under consideration and will take them home and let our updated Miss Mix equivalent make the decision. Little did I know that a single button can cost as nearly as much as a good Italian cold cut sub with hot peppers.

Part of how we're paying the updated Miss Mix (a friend who last made wedding dresses in the 80's in Hawaii) is to buy her a sewing machine. Her last sewing machine was bought in 1972, and barely did buttonholes let along automatic embroidery of little pine trees and the other wonders of which a modern entry-level Bernina is capable. I know NOTHING about sewing machines, other than that threading the ones we had in home ec in 1963 was a nightmare.

Luckily Miss Mix (real name: Debra Matteson) found an eager sewing machine salesperson who not only helped her select the machine, assured her it would do everything needed, but also rescued us from the horrible mistake of buying silk thread to sew silk. Silk thread cuts silk fabric. Who knew? So we turned in the silk thread I had carefully matched for some other stuff that looked the same to me, but is evidently very different.

She also made us give back the fusible interfacing and buy some organza instead that gets sewn instead of fused. What-

Jessica Weissman

ever. My head was spinning by this time, so we fled outside for a reality break...and ran into SHOES. I can see that our waterloo will be shoes.

Dinner calls. Details next time.

March 19, 1997

We are planning to send out reply postcards with the invitations. Louise the sometimes-very-observant noticed that one of the current USPS pre-stamped postcards features St. John's College in Annapolis, my alma mater, and the third oldest college in the US. Unfortunately, this particular design is just being phased out in favor of postcards picturing the FOURTH oldest college in the US (Harvard). I guess they're going in chronological order, or something.

So, we need to track down about 80 more SJC postcards.If any of you know how to order a particular design from the post office, or see any of these in your local post office, please let me know.

March 22, 1997

Through the kind offices of Alison Hendon we now have enough St. John's College postcards to use for reply cards. Through the unkind offices of Microsoft and Hewlett Packard and the vagaries of computer font substitution, we have approximately 75 drafts of the invitation, all of which but one are in the wrong font. The single one that's in the right font I have never been able to duplicate. I hate computers.

I get my first WLT costume fitting today. Can't wait. Our Miss Mix claims to have the jacket about 2/3 done. We'll see.

March 23, 1997

I've seen the outfits (I have been forbidden to call them "costumes" in the same transaction that allowed me to keep calling it the Weddinglike Thing) and they will be glorious!!!! My silk jacket is almost 2/3 done, with darts and one of the pockets attached. Somewhat to my surprise, the slubs or texture lines of the silk run horizontally, not vertically. Our Miss Mix is

Tales of the Weddinglike Thing

meticulous, matching the slub pattern precisely for the pocket flaps against the main jacket body. This apparently made the first pocket take nearly all of King Kong on tape for her to finish. I didn't know you could spend more than five minutes making a pocket, but what do I know? She says the next nine pockets and flaps will be faster (that's five on each jacket — one breast pocket, two fake flaps and two side pockets, all matched precisely).

We unfolded the lace, and discovered that it is edged with scallops, and the scallops are traced with beads. Because it was always folded double on the bolt, we hadn't seen this bonus feature before. So the scallops will form the upper edges of the v-necks of the bodice/vests. I also learned the difference between crepe de chine and regular thin silk (sorry about the missing diacritical marks on "crepe de chine", but ASCII-only email programs would be very upset if I put them in). We'll use crepe de chine to line the lace on the vests. Still no final decision in the button department, let alone the shoe department.

In the chuppah holder department, we now have all four people lined up to hold the poles. I've discussed the string quartet repertoire with the string quartet leader, and we'll make some decisions there soon. We're procrastinating dangerously in the tent department, I am ashamed to say.

Invitations go out this week, thanks to Alison Hendon whose friend who works at the P.O. got us enough St. John's postcards to use for reply cards.

Somebody else, who has legible handwriting, gets to address the envelopes and the postcards. Luckily.

March 24, 1997
TWO-TEA WEEKEND

Proving once again that events are not distributed uniformly in the plenum, I attended two Ladies' Teas this weekend, after several years of attending no teas at all. I look forward to several tealess years after this.

Jessica Weissman

THE FIRST TEA

The first was a wedding shower. Two of Louise's brothers have decided to follow her example and get married this spring. We held a shower for the fianceeee of one of them on Saturday. This was a tea shower, wherein you are supposed to bring a teacup that reflects your personality and taste as a gift to the near-bride, and then drink out of it after she unwraps and admires it. I had a lot of trouble finding such an object, and was disappointed to find that either Phyllis's friends were extremely ordinary or didn't try very hard to find the perfect thing.

And why not get Phyllis a cup that reflects HER personality rather than mine, I want to know. After all, she is the one who gets to drink from it in years to come.

Despite my whining, we all enjoyed the tea and the little sandwich things and the baked goods. Then we turned to conversation. A little background here: Louise comes from an extremely interesting family that was dysfunctional when dysfunctional wasn't cool. They're all okay about it now, but when you get more than two of them together, conversation inevitably turns to their fascinating mother, who went in nine short years from Republican Mother of the Year for their county to a steep alcoholic decline and eventual death.

The brother Phyllis is marrying is the one who made the coffin for their mother with his own hands (and a few tools). We got the story of how this gang of teenagers and very young adults persuaded the funeral home to let him do it, how they made sure the coffin would be big enough by taking turns getting in it (the pregnant one nearly got stuck), and how the oldest sister nearly died of embarrassment at the whole thing. Watching Phyllis's friends take all this in was definitely worth the price of admission. Phyllis, of course, had heard it all before.

THE SECOND TEA

The second tea was at a friend's house, held in honor of Spring for a bunch of happy middle-aged women, mostly old friends of mine. Some of them whom I rarely see had not yet

Tales of the Weddinglike Thing

heard about the WLT or met Louise, so I had to persuade them that my curmudgeonly self was doing all this voluntarily. The guests included another pair planning a WLT (luckily NOT for the same date), so we got to compare notes and giggle. Then we all got toasted. I've never felt to affirmed by my community (or so Betsy-ish, come to think of it) in my whole life.

SURREAL ESTATE MOMENT

The house next door to me is for sale, and had open yesterday, so I took a look. Nothing so weird as looking at your own third-story windows nearly on the level. Too bad I don't have twice my income, or I'd buy the thing and have one of the shortest moves on record.

March 26, 1997

A NEW METHOD FOR KEEPING ONE'S SLEEPING COMPANION AWAKE

In my insomniac career I have put up with tooth-grinders (it was my little sister and we were preteens so I could kick her awake until I fell asleep), snorers (too many to count) and talkers. I've even put up with someone reading ostensibly silently but saying "hmm" a lot. But NEVER, until last night, have I tried to fall asleep while someone hiccuped.

Hiccuping is just irregular enough to be infuriating, just loud enough to hear through the pre-dream fog, and is accompanied by bedclothes movement (if you're lucky) and actual mild bodily collision if you're not.

YIKES! Despite which, there is still

Jessica Weissman

MORE WLT PROGRESS

Louise got measured for her outfit last night, and reports that Miss Mix is in good spirits despite being a slave to pockets, and has my jacket NEARLY done. As Miss M is an optimist, I feel I should go check on this myself. She is also threatening to pick out the buttons by herself. A tempting offer, since I think I've filled my lifetime allowance of time spent in a fabric store.

Two different shower-events are in the works, one planned by my buddies the Reasonably Bright Girls and another by yet another chunk of Louise's family. The RBGs have promised that I don't have to wear a paper plate on my head or anything, but Louise's family has promised NOTHING. Nor is there an announced theme. I tremble in fear as to what this bunch will come up with.

The RBGs I can trust...or can I?

April 1, 1997

We have seen our Dream House. It is a handsome bungalow in the heart of Takoma Park, near Louise's favorite sister and not far from one of her brothers. It has a front porch with a swing, a perfect layout downstairs, three bedrooms upstairs, a brick sunken patio, a grape arbor with some hardy grapevines that should survive our non-gardener care, and a lot of lovely dark wood trim inside. There is an alcove in the back, just behind the living room/dining area, with windows and a window seat and just the right space for a couch and a lot of books. Louise's carpenter brother will build a wall of bookshelves for us, and that will be that. The layout will work nicely for entertaining.

It's probably going to be cold in the winter as the lovely mullioned windows are a bit leaky even with their storm windows over them. There is no central AC. But I can tell it is going to be home.

Tales of the Weddinglike Thing

April 3, 1997

Just a quick (yeah, right) note to say that we have a contract on the Dream House, at the price we wanted. All that remains is to figure out the settlement date. If my buyer cooperates, it will be April 28th. If he doesn't, or, rather, if his lugubrious yet strangely powerful girlfriend Heather doesn't, we wait until May 28th.

At the negotiations we found out that the Dream House roof was indeed only 3 years old — Louise, who has quite sound instincts about roofs (gotta wonder what primitive ancestral capacity useful to our hominid forbears evolved into this) thought it was okay on sight, but she didn't intuit just HOW new it is. Also new copper piping and a newish boiler. Wow. And we thought it was simply gorgeous, spacious, graceful and well situated.

I'm thrilled. The whole Betsy and Joe house-hunting story ran through my mind all the time we were negotiating, of course.

April 7, 1997

We got to inspect the Dream House last night, and it has a few things the owner needs to fix. Should work out fine, though. Move-in date will be May 28th. So we'll come back from the post-WLT trip, stay with friends for one day, and move into the new home. We plan, being grownups, to pay people to pack and move. A convenient niece of Louise's will supervise the process while we are gone.

I love it even more, having gotten to spend three hours wandering around while the inspector made jokes. The Secret Room in the basement contains lots of cans of paint and a few ladders.

The lovely molding and windows and window seat (!) are all of oak and chestnut. The brick patio is even nicer than I remembered, with the bricks set in an interesting curve. The wooden pillars on the front porch are square and hollow, and a door could be cut in one of them to make a secret hiding place.

Jessica Weissman

There's one big tree and one small pine, and some miscellaneous bushes and a few bulbs and some ground cover. Nothing high maintenance in the yard.

I will be ecstatic, having all that space. A whole room just for books and chairs! A separate whole room for computers and workspaces!

I hope to report on last weekend's family wedding (highlight: the brother entrusted with the rings lost them in the lining of his coat, necessitating a longish pause in the ceremony) and on WLT progress as soon as I finish analyzing all extant SGML editors for the current client.

April 14, 1997

Well, I suppose this is progress. I am now actually registered at Crate and Barrel. Registering involves trailing around the store carrying a metal clipboard and writing down the stock numbers of things you might want to hint explicitly to your friends that you want. Simultaneously other people on the same mission are wandering around with clipboards, and OTHER people are wandering around with printouts that are the results of the first set of people and their clipboards.

C&B splits up categories like glasses and plates and such in many places in the store, so you have to wander around a LOT to see all the different types of, say, cute salad plates, before making a choice..

I get to repeat this at Williams Sonoma, where there is far more that I actually would like and don't already own an equivalent of.

AND we have endured The First Shower. I am sad to report that my trusted RBGs betrayed my trust. While they did not make me wear a paper plate on my head, having all sworn they wouldn't, THEY DID MAKE ME WEAR A PLASTIC PLATE INSTEAD! The sophistical dweebs! They created a rather nice hat with a variety of flowers carefully cut out of wrapping paper, added a wax paper veil and a mock bouquet, and made us take turns wearing the resulting ensemble. I am

Tales of the Weddinglike Thing

not sure I can afford to buy the negatives of all the photos taken. Louise tossed the mock bouquet, which was caught by the RBG most in the market for a new spouse.

I now live in mock dread of the next shower.

April 20, 1997

So, we have now lived through the second and last shower. This one was family, Louise's friends and a couple of my friends who could not make it to the WLT itself and wanted an alternative. Fine food and good company.

My heart sank when I saw the white paper accordion bells on the front door, but it was just tokenism in the embarrassment department. After that it was all coasting, especially after Louise's friend Sheryl, a 6-foot blonde former stewardess, devoted herself in a fit of job nostalgia to keeping everybody's mimosa glass full. I guess if she could serve drinks from those big carts in those teeny aisles, she could do it in a small living room full of chairs and treacherous piles of wrapping paper.

One of the high points was watching my righteous friend Dr. Mary Hunt, a feminist theologian, tangle with a couple of Louise's friends who are deeply involved in new age philosophy but are extremely righteous about it underneath the new age veneer. I think they were disagreeing about the validity of theological speculation, but I tried not to listen too closely.

Finally everybody left but family, and we settled down to the obligatory end of party discussion of Louise's mother. For those who tuned in late, Louise comes from a very complicated family including one of those fatally attractive alcoholic mothers. They're all over it now, but they can't help talking about her. I picked up many additional details this time, including:

Johnny, the brother who made the mother's coffin, screwed up and made the handles slight too wide so they wouldn't fit into the cement vault. He had to trim them down with an ax and a chisel at the last moment. This was the mid-seventies, and he was going through a belated full hippie stage combined with a nascent Native American rights stage. The sight of a tall long-haired man in a bearclaw necklace, smelling of alcohol, walking into the funeral home with an ax in his hand probably scared the socks off the undertakers.

Then he tried to fight the gravediggers who wouldn't let him help dig the grave, because he wasn't in the union. The de facto head of the family at the time was a union engraver at the Washington Post, so he sided with the gravediggers.

Later Johnny tried to punch Louise because he didn't like a reference in the poem she read at the funeral.

What more could you ask for in a new family than high drama, all safely in the past? And I'm leaving out PLENTY.

April 28, 1997
DIGRESSION: NEW YORK

How can you tell you're in New York? When it's Passsover, and the cafeteria at the Federal building has a box of matzoh stationed next to the bagels and the 3 types of cream cheese.

This was a successful business trip, for once. The software I was teaching only blew up when users tried to enter data on buildings with apostrophes in the names (hard luck for the Tip O'Neill Building, but the Jacob Javits Building was okay). Due to schedule switching I couldn't meet any sistren this time, but hope builds for the future.

AND I got to have lunch with my college friend Robin and her husband and brother. All of them in their mid-40's to early 50's, with identical grey streaked ponytails. They all work in advertising, though Robin also publishes kid's picture books. She says, by the way, that although she advertises a famous pet flea remedy, you can just use diatomaceous earth and it works better. Good luck identifying which Famous Flea Products incorporate diatomaceous earth and which don't.

Tales of the Weddinglike Thing

WLT PROGRESS

Our Miss Mix and I took the final trip to G Street fabrics on Sunday, to pick out the buttons and the flesh colored linings for the lace vests, and to get some more thread. Evidently if you change your mind a lot and rip out the sleeves and reinsert them until they are perfect, you use up more thread than anticipated. The thread was the easy part.

We brought back all the buttons I'd been talked into buying one each of in hopes that I could learn to tolerate them, and traded them, plus lots of cash, for 34 varyingly iridescent glass buttons that "we" managed to select just before my powers of choice deserted me completely. So I knuckled under to the wisdom and taste of our assigned Button Lady and Miss Mix. If two such experienced selectors of frou-frou accessories believe that iridescent glass buttons aren't tacky then I guess they simply aren't tacky. Time will tell.

Then we went over to another part of the store to select the linings. Let me be the first to say that no cloth is actually flesh tone, any more than the Crayola now known as peach but formerly known as flesh matched any known human flesh. On top of which Louise and I have strikingly different skin tones (olive and Irish-pale). Miss Mix, perfectionist that she is, got EVERYBODY in the lining department, official Lining Ladies and hapless customers alike, to vote on which of several silk lining shades would work on me and which on the absent Louise. I pleaded the Fifth, then abstained. So we have two different shades, and anybody who doesn't like it can just talk with my legal representative. At least all the True Fabric People liked the lace – or maybe they were just obeying some form of Fabric and Notions Courtesy which dictates that you always admire anything another customer has already bought.

Jessica Weissman

So that's the end of it. My final visit to G Street Fabrics is now history, or at least biography. Or biomythography, to borrow a term from Audre Lorde.

Yours with a lungful of sizing and fabric dust

May 1, 1997

Well, eager readers, we've finally had our first serious WLT panic. We made a count, and it looks like more than 100 people are showing up. Louise and Mattie-the-cateress (a friend whose gift to us is being in charge of the food) had just gone to Price Club and other places to price out the food. They're going have to scale up. And it had better not rain, since no WAY will all those people fit under our token tent.

We've taken the foolish and risky step of mail-ordering candidate WLT shoes. They're low-heeled bone leather pumps with interesting little bumps on them — the royal blue were out of stock. When Our Miss Mix heard about them she immediately offered the services of her pal who dyes leather shoes, so I think we have made a Fashion Faux Pas in her eyes.

We have the penultimate fitting on Saturday morning for the lace vests and non-lace skirts. Stay tuned.

BOOKSTORE ELEGY

One of the cooler bookstores of Washington goes out of business tomorrow. Sidney Kramer Books, which originally specialized in dry books about economics and politics and area studies but then made a fatal attempt to become a more general bookstore, held a spot between the World Bank and the General Services Administration buildings downtown. For its first decades it did a worthy job as Policy Wonk Central, but lost its focus somewhat in later years. When a couple of the more serious big chain bookstores opened up within two blocks, and it was doomed.

Since I was in the neighborhood anyway due to a bungled attempt to pick up some orthotics, I stopped in and got some high minded serious non-bestseller poetry books at closeout discounts. Not to mention a couscous cookbook I've had my

Tales of the Weddinglike Thing

eye on for a while. I wonder whether someone will give us the couscoussiere I registered for, so we can make truly authentic couscous on those days when we have five or six hours to spend on dinner preparation.

They're selling off their serious, high-minded-looking wooden display cubes, too. All the customers were apologizing for not buying more books earlier, and the staff was taking it all in, graciously.

They were around for 51 years. Ah well.

May 5, 1997

The skirts are done, and Our Miss Mix is threatening to keep whichever one fits her better. Luckily she is between our two sizes, so this is a hollow threat. Louise's jacket, which OMM farmed out to a professional tailor friend who owes her a favor, is done too. But hers has only three pockets; mine has all four, including the fake pocket over the breast pocket. Mine will be done real soon now, and it's a nicer color anyway. So there. The lace bodice/vest things are next, but they are (supposedly) simple to make.

May 7, 1997
CEREMONY DESIGNED AT LAST

We met with the celebrant last night and figured out the liturgy — we are modifying the standard Jewish ceremony in a couple of ways, and using freely modernized translations of many of the blessings. We will drink from wine cups held by each other, and then each of us will offer the wine to relatives and friends of the other. We will use nonstandard wording for the ring exchange (the original involves "The laws of Moses", which just doesn't ring right). Each of us will compose her own wording for this, and her own wording for the response, following an agreed upon non-embarassing formula but keeping the wording secret until The Actual Moment.

Some of the Seven Blessings, for which we are using updated wording, will be read by friends and family members.

And the final pronouncement (you know, the one that usually begins "by the authority vested in me") will be replaced by a graceful Native American formulation about the two persons with one future life. The other place where we will honor Louise's ancestry is to have the welcoming blessing incorporate one of the Native American blessings that refers to the directions, or compass points.

She's about 1/16th Penobscot, the rest Irish Irish Irish. The ceremony incorporates no bow in any Celtic direction, I'm sorry to say.

Then we exit for our ten or fifteen minutes alone together, while the assembled company attacks the two identical buffet tables. No receiving line. No dumb wait for official pictures. No program, though we will have the blessing that everybody gets to say printed up on little cards (the Shechecheyanu in Marcia Falk's beautiful translation,). We'll use some genderless God language and some feminized God language.

SHOES

Now for the important stuff. The light mail order pumps with the ostrichy bumps just don't fit Louise. So we will have to waste a chunk of Saturday buying shoes in person. Eeeeeek! And my jacket still lacks a right sleeve. There are ten days or so left. I expect Miss Mix will be working on that at the last moment. I hope I'm wrong.

No serious panic yet, despite all. I THOUGHT I lost my purse last week, but it turned up in a part of my office I never put it down in and never look in. It was presumed lost overnight, which gave me all the panic I need for a while.

May 10, 1997

It's 8 days away, and we have finally hit full panic mode. I have a list of 22 things to do, mostly small ones, and there are not enough minutes in the day. Louise chose to sleep until 11:30 this morning, cutting out plenty of good panicking and phoning hours, but I have forgiven her.

Tales of the Weddinglike Thing

EEEEK! We have to buy a plastic wading pool to use to hold drinks and ice, gather plastic trash cans from various people to hold trash and recycling, catch up with the string quartet to finalize the music selections, and do a million other small and large things in eight days. One of which I will probably have to spend in Boston doing some teaching.

On the other hand, we had a shoe miracle. We have found medium-heel Italian velvet pumps in iridescent blue-green velvet. They match the skirts precisely, though one shade darker. They were in the clearance rack of a large shoe warehouse place. Who would have thought that such shoes:

1. existed
2. were available in 9 wide
3. were on sale for $20 a pair
4. are comfortable enough to wear for the half-hour critical time (we'll put on something else after that for extended partying)

And who'd have thought I would wear such a thing! What love does....

We figure that my mother found them for us from the beyond — it took her a while because discount shoe warehouses didn't exist back in 1966 and she had trouble steering us to one. She's probably laughing her head off — last time she took me clothes shopping I was an extremely resistant teenager. Last legacy of a bargain-hunting elegant fashion plate. One could select far worse traits in a mother.

Now it's Louise's mother's turn — maybe she'll find us a good discount on wine and beer.

May 12, 1997

Whew! the panic is lessening. On Saturday afternoon, for my sins, I was dragged into this place called Costco, formerly known as the Price Club. It's a warehouse/membership superstore, where you can find hammocks and grass seed next to cases of beer and boxes of croissants. Someone had misguidedly thought that I should personally check out the beer and wine choices and prices. This was a major misapprehension. Needless to say, I now have my vision of the negative afterlife. I plan to be VERY VERY good so I am not sent to Price Club when I die.

We've re-inspected the site and done a layout plan (the room where we spend the 15 minutes alone together must be cleared of 53443 toys and a little dog hair, otherwise everything will be fine), tried on the nearly-completed outfits (gorgeous; made us both tear up a bit as we remembered WHY we are doing this ridiculous logistical marathon), and gotten vest fittings. Our Miss Mix is attempting to convince us that there will be no fabric scraps left over. This is nonsense. She is still trying to convince us that she should be allowed to keep one of the skirts.

THEN she decided to try makeup on me. She wears exquisite and elaborate makeup daily. Her mother does too, even when camping, even when they have to put it on at 6:30 a.m. just to go out in the woods. I have witnessed this. It's mildly surreal to sit up at 6:30 and discover that you're the only person in the room not making faces into a mirror and waving little sticks at her cheeks and eyes.

Anyway, after her ministrations even I looked exquisite and elaborate.

Except that she kept asking me questions about which kind of lip liner I wanted. Finally I convinced her that I had absolutely no idea or basis for making a choice. It was a little like the time one of my colleagues (nicknamed the Feral Programmer) got away from us and asked the client whether he favored data warehousing over real-time data replication.

So one of our friends will be drafted to help me put the stuff on a few minutes before curtain time. Wish them luck!

Seriously, folks, the panic is lessening. The weather is holding well. I may yet survive this!

Tales of the Weddinglike Thing

May 13, 1997

We have 129 acceptances as of last night. Seven of them are children. A few are dubious for actual attendance. It had better not rain. The yard is big enough, but the tent plus the house will be a tight fit for that many.

Everything is coming together. I finally figured out why Louise was resisting getting more wine as there were more people on the list. She was using the term "wine" to refer to "the good chardonnay that's mainly for the toast". I was using the term "wine" to refer to "all the wine, INCLUDING the stuff for the toast and the second-string chardonnay and the red wine and everything". I'm okay with not encouraging people to drink much, but it is Not Okay to run out of wine at a wedding.

The one sticky spot is the music. Suddenly the leader of the string quartet is unavailable by phone at either of her numbers. Is she avoiding me? Is she in trouble? Is she busy graduating? I hope to know before Saturday.

Now for the very good news. Louise's Aunt Pat, her charming mother's less charming but steadier younger sister, is coming along with many of her children. Said children are Louise's double first cousins, two sisters having married two brothers. All four are reliably reported to have asserted, loudly, to their spouses that they married the wrong sibling. At any rate, a major reconciliation has been effected in the family, and a goodly sampling of The Other Parkers are coming.

Amazing!

May 14, 1997

So, Maudiacs, nearly all the big items are checked off the list. The music leader finally called me — the number I had been frantically beeping her on doesn't work during the day when she is at work. The alternate number where I had been getting an irritable person who wrote down messages was from an old business card, and listed an old roommate's phone. No wonder. So it is too late to have my precise dream music, but what we have will be fine.

Jessica Weissman

The rehearsal dinner is planned, costed and specified — a nicely decorated Thai place with a fixed menu avoiding shrimp and pork. The rehearsal itself is planned out, and Louise's born-again brother who can't/won't attend the wedding is going to come to the rehearsal and dinner to meet my family and offer his congratulations. This is the end result of some extremely delicate negotiations.

Best of all, we have a larger tent. The tent guy from the party place went to check out the location at last, and couldn't figure out why we wanted such a small one (16 by 20 isn't small in my book, but it is in his). Turns out we got bad advice from someone at the party place who doesn't usually do tents. So we are getting a 30 by 20 tent, with almost twice the space, for only $15 more. Good thing he took the initiative.

We should now be okay, sort of, even if it rains, which it won't.

Louise went out and bought the wading pool/drink holders and some kind of rollout plastic stuff for us to step on in a makeshift aisle (AND instructed the person running things day-of about precisely when to roll it out). I spent the early part of the evening on the phone reassuring various guests that we had indeed gotten their RSVPs, talked one niece into taking the train from Newport News (miraculously the train schedules work out perfectly) and making minor decisions for the friend who is doing the catering. I envied Louise being away from the phone until I realized that SHE had to go to Toys R Us to get the wading pools

At least it was late enough that most of the tiny consumers who make that place a gauntlet of frustrated but fully-expressed desire were asleep at home.

Finally I tottered over the computer for a guilty pleasure. I'm giving one of my sisters the Monty Python and the Holy Grail computer game as her bridesmaid trinket. Now I don't usually play these things, but this one is funny and relaxing.

Just when I settled in, Our Miss Mix called, wanting me to come over for a vest fitting and keep her company as she cut and sewed. So, being weak-willed yet eager to get away from the telephone, I gave in.

It was fine until she tried to ask me whether it was okay if the lace scallops on the two vests were on different sides. At the best of times I have trouble picturing things like this. I swear I gave an answer, but apparently I never managed to move my mouth so that she heard the answer.

So she woke me up, it was midnight, and I drove (carefully) home.

Where I found a few more phone messages, including a 3-minute description of just what kind of disposable diapers I should buy for my niece. No, my sister can't bring them on the plane. I just hope I get it right, as it is genuinely important for Rachel to have the diapers she is used to. Plus we do not want my sister to have ANYTHING to hold over me, even something so arcane as inadequate diaper-selection skills.

Ah well. I've decided not to answer the phone tonight (HA!) and get some sleep. Truly, everything is handled that can possibly be handled ahead of time. I will concentrate my vibe-power on NOT having to make Debra Didn't Finish T-shirts to wear instead of the vests (Debra is Miss Mix's real name). I will concentrate my good will on finding a better wording than "Debra is Finished" for the congratulatory T-shirt we plan to give her.

Not that this woman would actually wear a T-shirt in public.

Thanks for the various good wishes we have received.

May 15, 1997

Well, we're holding steady at about 130 acceptances, with one person taking "and family" to mean that she could bring her mother in law. To be fair, this is a close cousin of Louise's and the mother-in-law is generally beloved. But really! We may be reduced to turning water into, if not wine, then at least seltzer water mixed with juice. We hit 135, but some people, such as the woman 8 months pregnant with twins, are calling to back out. We've got the diapers for my sister (no, no, not what you think! It's for her kid), the wedding-party baubles for all but one of the wedding party, and the wading pools and plastic ware.

Today I have to finish most loose ends at work, meet Miss Mix for what she claims will be the last jacket fitting before inserting the lining (Good news: my jacket now has both sleeves), meet the string quartet leader at Metro to give her the checks and a set of cues, and then go home and make some stir-fry for dinner. We're trying to use up all the food in the house rather than moving some of it, which makes for strange wokfellows.

Best news: the five-day forecast now stretches unto Sunday. No rain is predicted though it will be getting warmer. It's probably premature to say that you can ease off on your weather-related Maudvibes, but things are looking good. And there's nothing on the schedule tonight except for probably massive incoming phone calls.

On the other hand, WHAT'S LEFT FOR ANYONE TO CALL ABOUT? Don't, please, answer that question.

May 16, 1997

As we count down toward the Sunday 2pm time for the WLT, the good parts are starting. I'm off work today, visiting Land of 1000 Errands (apologies, Wilson Pickett); my family arrives on three different planes at two different airports tonight.

Last night I met the string quartet leader in the Metro on the way home and we got the music set — lots of nice things, none of which I had imagined ahead of time. And they found the Gershwin arrangements for string quartet! Hearing those will make my father very happy.

I got a copy of the nominally final guest list faxed over from Louise's niece who is handling the responses — it's a masterpiece of impressionistic spelling. Good thing we know our friends' names or we would have no solid idea who is coming.

Today I have to fetch two cases of wine from 13 miles away (never mind that they are only about $15 cheaper per case than a place 2 miles away; the discount was negotiated as a sidebar

Tales of the Weddinglike Thing

to a burgeoning romance between the caterer-friend and a relative of the storeowner, and who am I to mind an extra half hour of driving on Errand Day?). Then I pick up the last wedding party baubles, clean my car and house, find a navy-blue 28-inch half slip for Louise, try yet again to get the chimney-repair guy on the phone, call Miss Mix to keep her on task, stop for a chin-wax on the way to the airport, and meet my baby sister at the airport.

My family are all displaying their variegated styles of pre-event worry and misplaced precision planning. One sister, as previously recorded here, gave me minute directions about some supplies to buy for her toddler. The other sister kept asking for a complete schedule for Saturday and assurances that she wouldn't have to drive anyplace. My father wanted minute and exacting directions to the train station where he is to pick up my mother's cousin, including foolproof directions to an unmistakable pickup point that she could find from inside the station and he could find in the car. All this via long distance phone, mixed with some discussion of the precise scheduling for converging on the new house for a showing.

My brother-in-law wanted minute directions from the subway to the motel and the name of a funky breakfast place where he could meet his former guitar teacher.

But NOBODY is willing to decide ahead of time where we will meet on Friday night or where and when we'll eat. This tiny detail they want to play by ear. I'm just glad I set things up so I get an hour alone with my baby sister before the deluge. And we probably won't spend ALL of it at the Beanie Baby stand in the airport.

Yours in the calm before the (most welcome) storm.

May 18, 1997

Well, one might ask, what is she doing in her office at 6:30 on the morning of her WLT-day, typing email?

BECAUSE HER HOME PHONE IS OUT! This happened sometime between 3pm Friday when I phoned Louise to give her the wording for the engraving on one of the wedding party baubles and 7pm when my baby sister and I tried to phone the hotel where the rest of the family is staying to see if they'd arrived.

No way could I wait around Saturday afternoon for the repair person to come, so somebody else is going to have to handle this for us so that we have a functioning phone for the two days next week we spend in the house before moving.

Maybe it's a blessing in disguise, ensuring no one could bug us by phone for last-minute decisions.

Anyway, after completing ALL scheduled errands on Friday I collected my baby sister Liz from National Airport, where what was a Beanie Baby stand three weeks ago is now a Wheeled Luggage sales stand. Are there that many travelers who arrive at the airport with their stuff in paper bags that a luggage stand can do any business?

After some fuss during which I had to adjudicate whether Liz's being ill from the plane ride was more or less incapacitating than Rachel our toddler niece being asleep at last after HER plane ride (I finally had to put it in words of one syllable: LIZ IS SICK. SHE CAN'T MOVE YET. WE HAVE TO EAT HERE, NOT IN SOME NICE SPOT YOU FOUND IN A GUIDEBOOK), we had a gourmet family supper of Ledo Pizza and Boston Chicken in the hotel room.

Next morning, after several complex logistics-based conversations, the three sisters took off for our massages. When we got there, it turned out that Miss Mix, who also does massage, was feeling ill and couldn't do them. I think she just wanted the time to finish the vests, since she didn't seem all that sick to me.

The outfits are supposed to be done by 10:00am today. Miss Mix's mother is here for the WLT, and she can be trusted to keep her daughter on task. You'd think a seamstress would know that beads break sewing machine needles, and get herself an extra supply..

Tales of the Weddinglike Thing

The upshot being that filled the massage slot with a 3-sisters ritual trip to Nordstrom, where my sisters pestered me for judgments on the relative cuteness of toddler outfits and then browbeat me into buying a couple of outfits for the post-WLT trip. Not that I actually minded. The outfits are seriously cute and nothing I would have looked at on my own.

At 1pm (more logistics; don't ask), we all converged on the Dream House, where the brother-in-law real estate agent let us into the house so everyone could take a look. Louise's brother who lives nearby dropped over, ostensibly to get us to decide which suit he should wear to walk her down the aisle but actually to show off the pictures from his wedding a couple of weeks ago in Las Vegas (no, no, not like that; his wife's family lives there).

We hung out until 2:30, got people into various cars going to various destinations after negotiations that would have made the entire graduating class of the Famous Diplomat's School proud.

The rehearsal was fine, except that it was followed by 15 minutes of competitive direction-giving to get all the cars from the rehearsal/WLT site to the restaurant. I picked the restaurant because it has the best Thai food in DC and looks pretty, unlike most Asian restaurants in this area. I did not pick it for ease of finding.

We ended up in a car caravan anyway. Have you ever tried to lead a five-car caravan on a Saturday afternoon down a road lined with strip malls, where many many people want to cut in your little convoy? And not all stoplights can be counted on to last through five cars?

The dinner was everything I wished for — my sister loved her present, a battered old copy of Beverly Cleary's Sister of the Bride. My other sister loved her Monty Python game. Louise's family were happy with their variously engraved items.

And now, all we have to do is hope that Miss Mix finishes those (#$*)!!# outfits.

Jessica Weissman

The weather will be spectacular today — hazy sunshine for maximum thermal comfort and slow ice-melting.

My heart is full. I will see, and write to, all of you in about ten days.

Thank you for coming with us on this journey of a lifetime.

Tales of the Weddinglike Thing

The WLT Itself

May 18, 1997

Report from Sally Hand, one of the guests:

The day was beautiful, not a cloud in the sky. The temperature was in the low 70's, so nature cooperated. The service and reception were held in the back yard of some of Jessica and Louise's friends. The hostess is due to deliver a baby next month, her third, so we did not see much of her. The host was in charge of the very large dog and his two daughters. (The eldest was the flower girl.) So Louise really ran the show.

Guests came from as far away as Seattle and London, everyone was so nice. I met the sister from Omaha and Jessica's Dad. I went to the wedding with Jessica's next door neighbor, a woman who will soon be joining the Betsy-Tacy fan club, if I have anything to do with it.

To set the stage, the backyard is fenced by the largest trees and one large rhododendron. All that green and the little bit of lilac were so wonderful. All that kept going through my mind was the old song "I know a Green Cathedral" (Anyone, what is the next line?, I stayed up half the night trying to remember?) There were five rows of chairs and then the rest of us stood in the back. The procession started with the minister.

She is an ordained Congregrationalist, but performed a "Jewish" wedding, complete with the Hebrew blessings. Then the chuppah holders arrived. The chuppah was a flowered tablecloth I had made held up on bamboo rods.

Next a small girl strewed rose petals on the "carpet". The best man and the maid of honor were next. Finally the brides arrived. Jessica was first and was escorted by her father. She looked wonderful, in her purple raw silk jacket, teal blue beaded lace vest and teal blue chiffon skirt.

Jessica Weissman

Her makeup was done to perfection and I have never seen her look so happy. Her Dad was beaming too.

Next came Louise on the arm of her brother in the same outfit except that her jacket was the same teal blue that made up Jessica's outfit. They looked wonderful together and even found wonderful velvet shoes to go with everything.

The service was almost the same service that my sister had at her wedding even down to the Seven Blessings. To include more people in the service, friends and family were each asked to recite one of the seven blessings that are said at a "traditional" wedding. The changed some of the wording to fit the situation but they kept the original Hebrew. They exchanged rings, I only got to see Jessica's, hers is a round opal in a wonderful setting. I am not very good at describing jewelry, but it looks wonderful on her hand.

While they exchanged rings, they exchanged vows that made me cry, (Okay I cried at Ben's Bar Mitzvah too.) but they were very touching and really represented how both Jessica and Louise feel. At the end of the service they both broke a glass and although I am one who believes that there are male and female rituals it really seemed to fit. After the glasses broke the string quartet broke out in a rendition of Simim Tov and Mazel Tov and every one proclaimed Mazel Tov. In deference to Louise's beliefs she did cross herself at the end of the service. I wasn't sure how holy I was going to view this service but it was one of the nicest and holiest services I have ever been to. These people really love each other and will spend the rest of their lives together.

At the reception Jessica's Dad did two things that were very special. The first was that he went around with a tape recorder and had every guest tape a statement to the brides. The second was his toast. He said he had arrived that day with three daughters and that he was leaving with four. (tears again) This was an even more important toast than you can imagine since Louise and I had a long talk about how important it was for both of them to have their families take part in the wedding

Tales of the Weddinglike Thing

and I was sort of shocked that any family member would not be there. (Don't you love your children and want them to be happy? If the found the right person, shouldn't you support them?)

The food was wonderful. They had lots of everything, the centerpiece was on each table was a baked salmon and of course it couldn't be a wedding without smoked salmon as well. Lots of fruit, cheese, bread a wonderful pasta salad with sun-dried tomatoes and pine nuts. They even had an assortment of wedding cake. I believe one of Louise's nieces made the cakes.

Well what did I forget, oh yes the Ketubah. In an Orthodox Jewish wedding this is the real deal. This is the contract between the two families stating how they will each support the couple. The families each have to sign and there has two be at least two witnesses that are not members of either family. Jessica and Louise had an artist friend design theirs. It is a tree in the background and purple writing. What they did was have everyone who attended the wedding sign the Ketubah, sort of like what you do in a Quaker wedding were everyone signs. It will been framed and hung in their new home.

It was very special and I was very honored to represent this list there

May 26, 1997

Well, we're back from the post-WLT trip, and about to face the packer/movers tomorrow and the real estate settlements the next day. During this brief interlude, what better thing to do than read 200 accumulated emails and let my cyber-friends know how it all went? I'm reading email at my office, as my phone did not miraculously fix itself while we were gone.

Anyway, it was delightful to have Sally's account to read. Almost like being there myself!

What Sally couldn't tell you is that I spent the morning of the WLT sitting on a bench, waiting for the phone repair people who never came.

Jessica Weissman

Why waiting on a bench? Because the only way to get into my apartment building is to phone one of the inhabitants from the front door. No phone, no entry. So I decided to stay calm and await them on the bench at the door, reading Betsy's Wedding for a little thematic comfort.

Louise decided to go look for a basket for the flower girl and the proper shade of stockings for me. I guess different people handle stress differently. Personally, I'll take sitting on a bench over driving around looking for stockings, but there's no accounting for taste.

Little did I know that she would stay out until just after noon. I was in a total panic for the last half hour, waiting for her. I didn't know whether the dresses were finished, I didn't know whether Louise's car had broken down, I didn't know whether she was having trouble finding the stockings, I didn't know WHAT was going on.

At precisely 12 noon I gave up on the phone repair people and went upstairs to select alternative outfits for both of us. I found these, wrote a terse and pointed note informing Louise that I had left for the WLT site with the alternative outfits, and clattered back down the stairs....where I ran into Louise. We yelled at each other out of nerves, Louise told me that the outfits had been finished at 11:30am (thank heavens for Miss Mix's mother, in from Michigan and able to help her daughter through the final stretch), and jumped in the car, still yelling, then laughing at ourselves for yelling.

When we got there, everything was fine. We were able to be polite to Miss Mix, who insisted on dressing us herself and putting on my makeup for me (sneaking in much more elaborate makeup than I had envisioned, but what the heck). Part of why she wanted to dress us was that my vest needed to be pinned together in front rather than buttoned. There were buttons on it, but no buttonholes. Louise's was totally finished, but she got a couple of pins just to keep me company and to have a better fit.

Tales of the Weddinglike Thing

Sally's account of the actual wedding is probably better than I could produce. One teeny correction: Louise and I each broke a separate glass.

Another teeny correction: Louise didn't actually run things that day. We had a friend doing that. And it was a niece of Louise's who actually made the cakes, with some last-minute assistance from other family members.

They were splendid visually and tasted good, too.

Something Sally didn't notice: I botched it by putting the ring on Louise's right hand - a mistake she graciously covered up. I put it right during the 15 minutes we spent by ourselves after the ceremony.

Something Sally couldn't know: the born-again brother who wasn't going to come to the wedding **DID** actually come. I'm not sure what changed his mind, but it was another small miracle. I respect the convictions that were keeping him away, but I'm very grateful that he found a way to attend anyhow. It was the best gift Louise could have gotten.

Best reported remark by a child attendee: "Which of those two brides is the Mommy?"

Best gift that we opened: an entire box, that's twelve reams, of paper. This from one of Louise's more literal-minded guy friends. There was this mysterious and EXTREMELY HEAVY box on the gift table. By special request of the people who own the house, we opened it, to find a lifetime supply of printer paper. Apparently he'd asked Louise what we wanted. She said that two writers could always use paper, thinking he'd find some nice special stationery or something. Little did she dream he'd come up with a case of printer paper. He's VERY good at following directions, Gordon is.

Second-best gift: a potted iris with a little card detailing how it needed to be watered daily. Just the thing to give two people who are about to leave for a week. Fortunately we found it some willing foster parents.

Jessica Weissman

So, thank you all for your vibes and good wishes. I'm sure you all helped the weather stay splendid and the day go smoothly. I wish you could all have been there.

Postlude

June 1, 1997

As a recently minted authority on the bliss of married life, I have to jump in with regard to whether being married is better than being single. Of course when one finds the right partner, being married is head and shoulders and piles of boxes above being single. But the pushing of marriage with the implicit promise that ANY marriage is better than being single is wrongheaded in my opinion (okay, IMHO). We've all known women who just wanted to get married, no matter what. Their second marriages tend to be much happier than their first ones.

Something like floating. While I was learning how to swim all those decades ago, we first had to learn to float. I kept propelling myself through the water by kicking and thrashing, and thinking that was floating. When I finally caught on to how to float, it felt totally different.; the water bore me up without any flailing. No way to mistake the one for the other.

Similarly with partnership/marriage. I've had a few prior partners over a lifetime, and thought that the kind of grumpy and distant strife mixed with a few nice things was How It Was Supposed to Be. Imagine my surprise when I found myself "floating", first with Sue and then later with Louise.

THAT was better than being single. Nothing previous had been, if I were to be honest.

I must go back to emptying boxes. I've got my computer set up at last, but no chair to go with it, and thus am typing this sitting on the floor with a cat lying next to me demanding attention.

June 7, 1997

And now for the guaranteed non-embarassing, essential-privacy-preserving description of the WLT postlude.

Jessica Weissman

Once the overzealous cleanup crew started stacking up chairs virtually while people were still sitting in them, almost all the guests left and we hung out for an hour or so with the crew (NOT the chairstackers, who were apparently eager to get out of there themselves).

Eventually we fled back to my apartment and collapsed.

Then got up the next day to take the train to New York where we had intended to spend a day sightseeing. But, as other wedding vets know, all we were capable of was collapsing in the hotel room after admiring its marble bathroom. I was nursing what would turn out to be a spectacular cold, and Louise was just tired.

The next morning we got ourselves up bright and early for the train to Saratoga Springs, after Louise had a little fit in the train station over spilling her tea on the floor and on her sleeve. New York, she says, can't even keep its subway clean. This is a true fact, I said, and refrained from pointing out in my trademark reasonable manner that there WAS tea to be had on the train even though it wasn't Real Tea. Eventually the little fit passed, and Louise watched the Hudson go by while I blew my nose an impossibly large number of times.

Saratoga is small and pleasant, though I am glad we were not there during the high season. We had a small suite in a fancy hotel.

One high point was taking a mineral bath in the Lincoln Baths. These are not the Roosevelt Spa, the fanciest one in the Gideon Putnam hotel, but they were old and traditional enough for all practical purposes. I felt positively Mrs. Main-Whittaker-ish as the uniformed attendant led me to my tub, dumped in the bottle of scented oil (an innovation for this year, updating the baths from their earlier pure-mineral state), and showed me where to hang my clothes in my private cubicle and the little cot where I could nap briefly after my tubtime was up. All up and down the row I could hear other mineral bathees giggling to themselves, softly, in deference to the signs requesting quiet (in English and Japanese).

Tales of the Weddinglike Thing

Newsflash: a mineral bath has lots of little clear bubbles, which cling to one in visually interesting places.

Saratoga features several terrific non-chain coffeehouses, where we took up residence during parts of each day. For you old-time folkies, the famous Cafe Lena where many people including Bob Dylan performed early in their careers is still going strong. Also several fine used bookstores and a public library with a sale room. We may have set a local record for proportion of honeymoon spent looking at used books.

Mineral water, by the way, tastes awful. I spent a while lurking near two of the drinking fountains in Congress Park. The one nearest the park entrance looks pretty, but the fine print on the sign says that it gives out water from the city water supply. The one beyond it is actual mineral spring water. Lots of fun to watch newcomers drink from the first tap, then walk eagerly up to the second one, only to sip and make a face, then either warn off their companions or allow them to share the experience.

More people warned than not, which is reassuring about the human race.

Six days of hanging around reading and walking and talking and eating was probably almost enough. We returned to one day of rest, followed by moving and real estate settlements. That's another story, which I will tell shortly.

July 4, 1997

What a day! NOW I know why we picked this house. The Takoma Park Independence Day Parade went right by our yard. We had what amounted to an all-day party, with people arriving in waves and departing in trickles, until at the end of the day nobody was left but our convalescent friend Lauren, who slept over on our couch, with a broom at her side to thump on the ceiling (our floor) if she needed assistance in the night. She'll go back to her own house later today.

So we had twenty-two people over at one time or another, starting just before the parade and ending with Miss Mix in the

Jessica Weissman

early evening. We have forgiven Miss Mix for dilly-dallying on the WLT outfits, and she has forgiven us for not dissuading her from taking on such a hard project.

People sat on the front porch and lined the yard during the parade. Later they spread all over the living room and the shady parts of the back patio and the porch, and jabbered and ate.

This was Some Parade. Started with politicians in 1957 Thunderbirds, continued with everything from a group in costume doing something like jigs (they'd stop, jig in place for a few measures, then march in jig time down the street for a few yards, then repeat). Jack the patriarch of Louise's family and an expert on everything but especially on all things Irish and Swedish, announced that it wasn't exactly an authentic jig but something else with a name I didn't catch. If it marches like a jig and is being done to The Irish Washerwoman played live by a costumed pickup band, I say it IS a jig. Riverdance it wasn't. Asphaltdance, maybe.

Continued with assorted groups of baton twirlers, ranging from teeny kids who could barely hold the batons, much less catch them, through bigger kids who could ALMOST do routines, to a total professional (male) twirler who could do ANYTHING with a baton and threw it higher than the rooftops and drew applause every time he posed in his tight little costume to await and catch the falling baton. He was leading a true brass band (not in matching uniforms, but they could PLAY). Imagine my surprise when I took a close look at the tuba player, only to discover that he was my co-worker the Feral Programmer. I didn't know he could function at 11 am.

This band brought up the rear. In between were kids on trikes with streamers, TWO reggae bands on floats with attendant dancers, THREE steel bands, a parody version of a Mardi Gras float (there's something hard to parody, but they did it, and I hope the parody was intentional), a troupe of trained dogs who heeled, sat and did some other dog tricks on command (followed by a pickup truck from the dog school,

Tales of the Weddinglike Thing

handing out cards), clowns, fabulous Caribbean and Asian dancers of several stripes, and groups advocating everything from veganism to the repeal of the law requiring the U.S. to go metric.

One of the guys in the Push Mower Drill Team stepped out of formation and mowed our verge (or parkway or whatever your dialect dictates you call that little grass strip between the sidewalk and the street). We tried to get him to come in and mow the rest of the yard, but he insisted on staying in the parade.

I had my usual pre-party panic, which alternated rapidly among Nobody Will Show Up, We Don't Have Enough Food, and We Won't Be Ready In Time (with a side order, directed at Louise, of Don't Do That, Do Something I Think Is More Important Right Now). I'm used to it by now, and can effectively ignore myself. Louise's version was quieter, consisting of sweeping the brick patio so her sisters wouldn't think she was a sloppy gardener. Never mind all the other evidence there wasn't time to get rid of in the fifteen minutes remaining before people were supposed to show up.

In the middle of the afternoon Lauren's caretaker of the day called to say that there was no one who could come sit with Lauren, and could she dump her with us? Of course, I said, and an hour later Lauren and her water bottle and her bag of painkillers and bread showed up and got ensconced in the comfy chair.

So we hung out in groups all over the house, patio and yard. Louise's sisters insisted on helping me in the kitchen so they didn't have to listen to their husbands talk to Lauren about real estate or hunting.

Both guys (the aforementioned Jack and Pete the real estate agent) are known to perk up and trot out their hobby horses for any new unrelated female. I had my turn during my extended family intake interview, and now it was Lauren's. She held her own without rancor, even on major painkillers.

Jessica Weissman

Good news: it was a success and we have plenty of yummy leftovers. Too bad I'm going to the convention and won't be able to do my full part in disposing of them. Bad news: we'll probably have to do it every year.

Throw me in the briar patch!

July 14, 1997

Marriage obviously makes people crazy. Just the other day I finally took the duplicate gifts we received back to Williams Sonoma, hoping to exchange them for additional settings of the perfect dishes we had selected. Imagine my agony when I saw NONE of the dishes there. The salesdroids thought they had been discontinued! I was in the dumps, devastated, etc. My entire vision of tabletop beauty and perfection lay in ruins. I thought we were going to have to bring back the two settings my adorable sisters had sent us, and get something else - something by definition inferior.

Today my Reasonably Bright Girl friend Mary Ann came by to compare notes on the Application on Which We Train people, and we went to lunch. We walked right past the Williams Sonoma near me, which is larger and staffed with brusque though competent people. In an effort not to walk more than a block in this heat, or, alternatively, Drawn by Fate, we went in.

Of course they had the dishes. I immediately fell on them with inappropriate cries of gladness. You'd have thought that Mary Ann had discovered the cure for cancer, or at least the cure for boredom. As I babbled on about how I should be worrying about world peace instead of dish patterns, the brusque counter lady just carried on with the transaction.

Not only that, the electrician finally returned our many phone calls, and we will have ceiling fans installed on Wednesday. This made me actually weep with joy.

Marriage — it's a wonderful thing.

Tales of the Weddinglike Thing

July 31, 1997

WHEN ETHNIC FOOD GOES TOO FAR

Last night I took a nap after work and let Louise cook. This goes better when I am asleep and unavailable for commentary and coaching. My major worry is gone now that we have separate sets of knives. Louise uses the mediocre Henckels set her brother gave us as a wedding present, and I use my lovingly assembled set of mismatched good knives.

She decided to use the last of my lovely gazpacho, with the seasoning corrected, that had aged for a couple of days to the perfect balance of vinegar and garlic against the vegetable tastes...

AND USED IT AS THE BASE FOR A CURRY SAUCE!

I have to admit it tasted decent despite this miscegenation of cultures, but I sure wish I had one more bowl of the gazpacho. Or am I just a control freak who's never lived with anybody two-legged until now?

Feel free not to answer that.

August 15, 1997

Kids, kids! We have found the answer, the magic dual keys that make it possible for two adults with fully developed but different cooking habits to share a kitchen without killing each other.

The first key, as I recently mentioned, is having separate knives. Louise uses a matched set of entry-level Henckels knives that were a WLT present, along with a knife block to house them. They're shiny and robust, and cannot easily be destroyed. Most importantly, they are not my good knives, which I have accumulated over many years, each perfect for its use, and not to be used for such things as cutting up tomatoes inside the can.

The second key is a ritual way to handle the overwhelming impulse to give kitchen advice. We have given up trying to cook together, since our methods and habits are so different. As much as possible, I stay out of the kitchen when Louise is cooking. When I can't help overhearing her doing something that goes against standard kitchen practice, or at least against everything I have learned, I no longer try to show her the better way. No, I do not. All I do is walk into the kitchen, say "You're doing that wrong," and walk right out again. This relieves my feelings, is over quickly, and after some negotiation is officially counted as a harmless neutral statement.

I commend this method to everyone. Feel free to use it without attribution, but do obtain the official Statement of Harmlessness first.

Tales of the Weddinglike Thing

Acknowledgements

Thanks first and always to Louise and to both of our families. My father, from whom I inherited a twisted sense of humor and thinning hair. My sisters Marion and Liz, who made my heart swell with pride and love when I saw them holding the chuppah poles. Not to mention their husbands Matt and Frank.

My niece Rachel, who is now a most impressive young woman. My niece Carrie and my nephew Andy, charmers both. My mother, who appears regularly when I look in the mirror, and who taught me that a job half done is a job undone.

Louise's sisters Chris and Kathy: I thought we would grow old together. Kathy's daughters Kateri and Chrissy who made the cakes, and the rest of Louise's many nieces and nephews and great-nieces and great-nephews.

Thanks also to the many subscribers to the Maud-L listserv, who were audience and inspiration. To Ada Lovelace, Charles Babbage, Alan Turing and the other inventors of the computer, who collectively saved me from work in some unfulfilling field. More particularly to the many inspired engineers who created the PLATO system, where I found my first online community. Also Bonnie Seiler, who taught me to program.

Thanks both practical and otherwise to my best friend and publisher, epic scholar Carolivia Herron.

About the Author

Jessica Weissman and Louise live in Silver Spring, Maryland in the successor to the Dream House, which is sunny inside and is much easier to maintain than their former Victorian bungalow. They had a fully legal wedding (referred to as the W) not long ago, this time in Tifereth Israel Congregation with Rabbi Ethan Seidel as celebrant.

www.ingramcontent.com/pod-product-compliance
Lightning Source LLC
Chambersburg PA
CBHW060507080526
44584CB00015B/1585